T0413676

MAGELLAN'S VOYAGE

BY DALTON RAINS

Apex is distributed by North Star Editions:
sales@northstareditions.com | 888-417-0195

Produced for Apex by Red Line Editorial.

Photographs ©: New York Public Library/Science Source, cover; Shutterstock Images, 1, 4–5, 18–19, 22–23, 25, 27; Chronicle/Alamy, 7; National Library of France, 8–9, 29; Stefano Bianchetti/Corbis Historical/Getty Images, 10–11; iStockphoto, 12, 13, 24; Photo Researchers/Science History Images/Alamy, 14–15; Jacques Descloitres/NASA, 16–17; Archive Photos/Getty Images, 20

Library of Congress Control Number: 2024941156

ISBN
979-8-89250-331-0 (hardcover)
979-8-89250-369-3 (paperback)
979-8-89250-442-3 (ebook pdf)
979-8-89250-407-2 (hosted ebook)

Printed in the United States of America
Mankato, MN
012025

NOTE TO PARENTS AND EDUCATORS

Apex books are designed to build literacy skills in striving readers. Exciting, high-interest content attracts and holds readers' attention. The text is carefully leveled to allow students to achieve success quickly. Additional features, such as bolded glossary words for difficult terms, help build comprehension.

TABLE OF CONTENTS

CHAPTER 1

SETTING SAIL 4

CHAPTER 2

HEADING SOUTH 10

CHAPTER 3

THROUGH THE STRAIT 16

CHAPTER 4

BACK TO SPAIN 22

COMPREHENSION QUESTIONS • 28
GLOSSARY • 30
TO LEARN MORE • 31
ABOUT THE AUTHOR • 31
INDEX • 32

SETTING SAIL

Ferdinand Magellan set sail from Spain on September 20, 1519. He led a fleet of five ships. He hoped to find a passage through South America. Then, he would go on to Asia.

This replica was made to look like the *Victoria*, one of Magellan's five ships.

The ships sailed west across the Atlantic Ocean. They had problems right away. People were upset that Magellan was working with Spain. The fleet had to avoid Portuguese ships.

TROUBLE AT SEA

Magellan was from Portugal. But he sailed for Spain. That made Portugal angry. Spanish crew members didn't like him, either. They didn't want to be led by a person from Portugal.

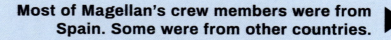

Most of Magellan's crew members were from Spain. Some were from other countries.

By December, the fleet had reached Brazil. They sailed down the coast of South America. Then they anchored for the winter.

FAST FACT

Near South America, Magellan started **rationing** food and water.

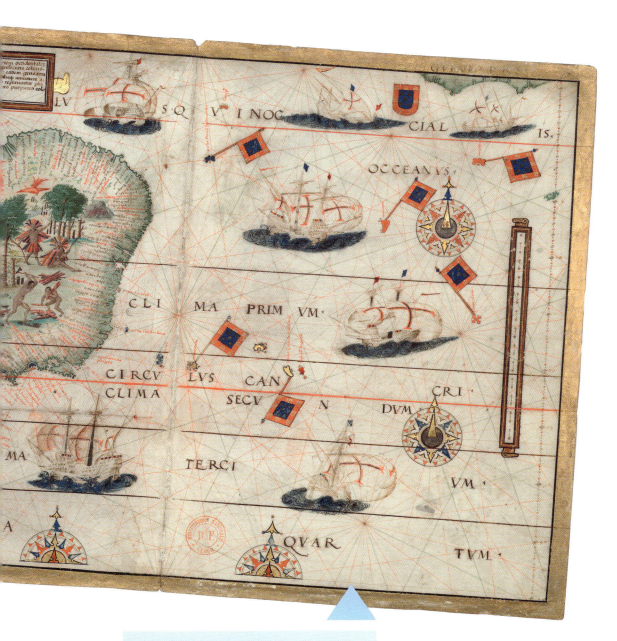

In the 1500s, Europeans had few maps of South America. They were still learning what the continent looked like.

CHAPTER 2

HEADING SOUTH

n April 1520, three of the ships' captains staged a **mutiny**. They tried to take over the fleet. But Magellan stopped them.

Magellan had two captains killed after they rebelled.
He left another in South America.

Magellan wanted to find a way to cross South America and buy spices in Asia.

Next, Magellan sent one of his ships farther down the coast. This ship wrecked in May 1520. The rest of the fleet sailed south in August.

OLD AND LEAKY

The ships in Magellan's fleet were small and old. Before the trip, the ships had been patched up and repaired. Still, more leaks sprung during the trip.

Magellan sent the *Santiago* ahead as a scout. The other four ships waited.

A storm pushed two of the ships toward land. The crews feared they would wreck on shore. But they saw an opening in the coast. It was a **strait**.

One of the ships left the fleet at the strait. The other three sailed through.

CHAPTER 3

THROUGH THE STRAIT

The strait had many narrow **channels**. Weather was stormy. Crossing took more than a month. Finally, the ships reached an ocean on the other side.

The Strait of Magellan is 350 miles (560 km) long.

Magellan thought they could cross the ocean in a few days. But it took more than three months. The crew ran out of food and water. Many people got **scurvy**.

The Pacific Ocean is huge and can have many storms. But its water was calm when Magellan reached it.

FAST FACT

Magellan named the ocean the Pacific. That means "peaceful."

In March 1521, the ships finally reached land. Then they sailed to the Philippines. Magellan got involved in local **conflicts** there. He died on April 27.

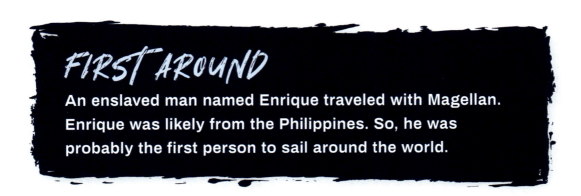

FIRST AROUND

An enslaved man named Enrique traveled with Magellan. Enrique was likely from the Philippines. So, he was probably the first person to sail around the world.

◀ **Magellan was killed by a poison arrow during a fight near the shore of Mactan Island.**

CHAPTER 4

BACK TO SPAIN

After Magellan died, the crew **scrapped** one of the ships. The other two kept sailing. Juan Sebastián Elcano became their leader.

Juan Sebastián Elcano was from Spain.

The Spice Islands were in Indonesia. People there grew and sold spices such as cloves and nutmeg.

The ships reached the Spice Islands in November 1521. From there, one ship continued west. It reached Spain on September 6, 1522.

FAST FACT

The crew started with about 270 people. Only 18 completed the trip.

The *Victoria* was the fleet's only ship that sailed around the world.

PACIFIC OCEAN

ATLANTIC OCEAN

PACIFIC OCEAN

INDIAN OCEAN

—— Magellan   —— Elcano   ✝ Magellan's Death

Magellan's **route** to the Spice Islands wasn't used often. Spain focused on land in South America instead. Even so, the trip helped people learn more about the world.

AROUND THE WORLD

In the 1500s, some people weren't sure the world was round. Sailing around the world proved it was. It also showed Europeans the huge size of the Pacific Ocean.

Even though Magellan died during the journey, he is remembered for his work as an explorer. ▶

COMPREHENSION QUESTIONS

Write your answers on a separate piece of paper.

1. Write a few sentences describing the main ideas of Chapter 3.

2. Would you like to travel around the world on a ship? Why or why not?

3. When did Magellan's fleet set sail from Spain?

    A. 1519

    B. 1520

    C. 1521

4. About how many years did the journey around the world last?

    A. less than two years

    B. nearly three years

    C. more than four years

5. What does **passage** mean in this book?

*He hoped to find a **passage** through South America. Then, he would go on to Asia.*

- **A.** a place to stay far from
- **B.** a person to talk to
- **C.** a way to get through

6. What does **staged** mean in this book?

*In April 1520, three of the ships' captains **staged** a mutiny. They tried to take over the fleet.*

- **A.** led a plan to act
- **B.** built a new ship
- **C.** watched and waited

Answer key on page 32.

GLOSSARY

channels
Stretches of water that connect two larger bodies of water.

conflicts
Times of fighting or disagreement.

mutiny
When people try to fight or disobey a group's leader.

rationing
Limiting the amount of something that people can have.

route
A way to get somewhere.

scrapped
Took apart or burned up a ship and left it behind.

scurvy
A painful sickness caused by not eating enough fruits or vegetables.

strait
A narrow passage of water that connects two larger bodies of water.

BOOKS

Morey, Allan. *Exploring the Deep Sea.* Minneapolis:
   Bellwether Media, 2023.

Petrie, Kristin. *Vasco Núñez de Balboa.* Minneapolis: Abdo
   Publishing, 2022.

Toolen, Avery. *Pacific Ocean.* Minneapolis: Jump! Inc., 2023.

ONLINE RESOURCES

Visit **www.apexeditions.com** to find links and resources
related to this title.

ABOUT THE AUTHOR

Dalton Rains is an author and editor from Saint Paul,
Minnesota.

INDEX

A

Asia, 4
Atlantic Ocean, 6

B

Brazil, 8

E

Elcano, Juan Sebastián, 22
Enrique, 21

M

mutiny, 10

P

Pacific Ocean, 16, 18–19, 26
Philippines, 21
Portugal, 6

R

rationing, 8

S

scurvy, 18
South America, 4, 8, 26
Spain, 4, 6, 24, 26
Spice Islands, 24, 26
storms, 14, 16
Strait of Magellan, 14–15, 16

ANSWER KEY:
1. Answers will vary; 2. Answers will vary; 3. A; 4. B; 5. C; 6. A